Love on the War's Frontline

ALSO BY AHMAD AL-KHATAT

The Bleeding Heart Poet
Gas Chamber
Wounds from Iraq
Roofs of Dreams

Love on the War's Frontline

**poems by
Ahmad Al-Khatat**

Poetic Justice Books
Port St. Lucie, Florida

©2018/2019 Ahmad Al-Khatat

book design and layout: SpiNDec, Port Saint Lucie, FL
cover image: ©2018, Julia Stuart

All rights reserved.

No part of this book may be used or reproduced in any manner whatsoever without written permission except in the case of brief quotations embodied in critical articles and reviews. Members of educational institutions and organizations wishing to photocopy any of the work for classroom use, or authors, artists and publishers who would like to obtain permission for any material in the work, should contact the publisher.

Published by Poetic Justice Books
Port Saint Lucie, Florida
www.poeticjusticebooks.com

ISBN: 978-1-950433-31-5

SECOND EDITION
10 9 8 7 6 5 4 3 2

For those that will appreciate my thoughts
and will connect to every word.

contents

Freedom on Earth	3
Due to My Color Skin	5
Again, and Again…	6
Because My Name Is	8
The Last Dialogue Before Killing Iraq	10
When Men Fall in Love	13
I Am Not a Poet	15
For the Very First Time	17
When Women Fall in Love	19
Colorless Dream	21
The Darkness and the Honey	23
Trump Sends Me Back Home	24
Yes, You Are a Terrorist	25
Await Your Reply	27
Help Me	28
What Will Remain	30
They Broke Me and Not My Heart	31
I Have One Kiss	32
Love in the War Frontline…	34
I Am Sorry Baghad	36

Love on the War's Frontline

Freedom on Earth

As one immigrant,
I always seek for
Freedom in exile.

I thought it was
In a can or frozen
Food, or a liquor.

So many confusions,
A few long questions,
Nobody has the facts.

I did math with letters,
I got Aero in percentage,
Joy versus grief in numbers.

I read the moon diary,
From the sun's rays to
Find the answers I need.

The freedom on earth,
It's becoming a nightmare,
Humans are now animals.

Teenagers are growing fast,
Adults are falling in depression,
Parents are walking separate.

Ahmad Al-Khatat

Keep up with the Kardashians,
Your dream to be Kim or Khloe,
Learn from their lives and live.

Freedom it's a new religion,
With a holy magazine of Playboy,
Awful fantasies are the prayer.

The pastor of the church weeps,
The nun becomes a stripper,
The sinner owns Jesus Christ.

The devil wins over freedom,
Fighters kill their own relatives,
No mercy to baby breast milking.

The poet writes and nobody reads,
The homeless attend all funerals,
And the poems die in bible verses.

The freedom on earth it's a miracle,
The magicians cannot change it,
As long as humans run carelessly.

Due to My Color Skin

I wake up alarming of
The sun begets me lightless.

I walk with one foot in
Grave, weak to find a mate.

I am a guard fencing
In an observant civilization.

I fail in cheerfulness,
Facing my tearful bleakness.

Due to my color skin,
Unmentionable as one being.

I write slant rhyme,
Amongst the loner villains.

I renounce old times,
On to my beloved generosity.

Ahmad Al-Khatat

Again, and Again...

The sorrows mood has started again,
And again, in my home from a long day.

I sat on a wooden chair like a little boy,
Talking to the four white old huge walls.

Staring at the dusty picture frames,
Singing to the missing ones in my home.

I stood up as if the soul is demanding me,
To dance with the presence of their spirits.

I was lying to nobody but my humble self,
But my eyes were honest when they wept.

Crying to see the world is turning me nuts,
For being heartless and emotionless to love.

All dancers were on the floor waiting on me,
To teach them a move to dance act again.

All musicians were in the studio waiting on me,
To sing them a song of nightingale to love again.

All the people were waiting in-line waits for me,
To write off my tears a poem, to die alone again.

Till I wake up with hands holding papers and a pen,
Feeling lost, it was the morning or the midnight time.

Wishing if my lips were wet or cleared off your lips,
To reorganize my sunshine from the same blue moon.

Where I can smile by breathing the roses of your pillow,
And cuddle the hanging stars in your stunning blue eyes.

You promised me to melt off your own visions upon my
Thoughts of this world who set me up as a leader in a war.

Melt your glows with the waves of tears down upon me
Grubby observations on a another attacking civilian land.

Melt your scents with cover me with your silky hair upon
My weak flesh, who sets to be taken by the king of death.

Melt your transparent heart between my heartbeats upon
My needs and desires for asking you to stay with me longer.

The day you walked away from my own joyful heaven,
Nothing seems to be the same anymore, but more miseries.

I can't see the blue skies any longer in the summertime,
But I see the raining clouds of autumn leaves on my hands.

Don't blame an atheist who said that he doesn't believe
In God, and so I am, I can't believe in love if you are not by me.

I have thrown my maps of my dreams, and my darkness keys.
Waiting for you in the middle of the beach alone
with tears alone.

Ahmad Al-Khatat

Because My Name Is

Because my name is...
I am not the son of Adam; my dad is the creator of Isis.
I am no longer a human being; I am just human killers.

I was born to love, respect, and forgive all the people.
Even if I had to walk with their guns behind my head.

My name defines kindness and being very friendly.
But nowadays it means I am a terrorist and criminal.

I have learned to write and educate myself with a pencil.
And share my love to the world with my pure drawing.

I always use a cheap knife to peel fruits and vegetables.
But when I cut my finger, they charged me for a crime.

You leaders had attacked my homeland and destroyed cities.
Because of your army, I am officially a stranger there.

Baghdad did not recognize me; I could not find my house.
Memories had stains able dusts, I lose my way to dreams.

I celebrate with your holidays, with a heart faithful intention.
Then why you agree to turn my holidays into a new funeral.

Even the clouds rain nothing but drops of the nature miseries.
And the rainbow lost his own colours between tears and pain.

The night in exile has been ignoring my daily conversations,
The moon still appears with the stars avoid hearing my prayer.

Because my name is...
I am on the edge of the danger, I am no longer allowed
   to love you,
Since I will be in the darkest prison, until the day I
   slowly die alone.

After all you may judge me because I am brown or
   black or yellow,
But for the love of our God why do all the animals not
   judge.

The mirror cannot read my face, nor see the blood
   from my heart.
My beliefs are my crime to you, so you did shoot the
   right man.

I refused to be a slave, and you have to point out that
   I am a terrorist.
I loved lots of women with a cross, with a David star,
   and a crescent.

Like an intelligent sister, like a respectful woman, and
   a loving wife.
And yet you are still behind my door, waiting on me to
   make a sin.

Ahmad Al-Khatat

The Last Dialogue Before Killing Iraq

Two gunmen were on the ground wounded,
Both have weapons without any courage to
Shoot one or another to death anymore.

None of them were talking but only praying,
Perhaps they both had similar beliefs in God,
And they both were raised from the same city.

The soldier from the national army started saying:
I wish to kill you like the way my brother died,
Leaving behind a wife and kids crying for him.

The Isis fighter responded without any fear:
I know you want to shoot me but I also desire
To know what happened to my missing parents.

The soldier said: your mother blew herself up,
When my mother was going to donate coins,
And buying a gift for your little sister's birthday.

The fighter said: and my father went to prison,
Stayed in jail for long months with cancer,
While he was innocent from all due charges.

The soldier cried and said with a high tone,
Your father destroyed my family in tiny pieces,
He bombed our house during my father's sickness.

<u>Love on the War's Frontline</u>

The fighter laughed and said that wasn't your
Home, it was my grandparents' house to us
And your family stole it without an intention.

The soldier: but your grandparents' burnt down,
My grandparents' tiny cottage and the farm too,
And left them poor till they died poor and miserable.

The fighter: do you remember my beautiful sister,
She was assaulted and abused by your brother,
Who ended up raping her till she died innocently.

The soldier laughed: you don't recall everything:
Your sister she died after she betrayed my sister,
To your men whom they tortured till her last breath.

The fighter with fears: is your brother still alive,
Cause I think I have killed him with cold blood knife,
He died and said you will kill me after his funeral.

The soldier faced down: will we stop creating
More bloody rivers from north to west of Iraq,
Somehow, we pray and we kill like a human Satan.

The fighter with fears: will we be forgiven or
We will die like sheep in the middle of the desert,
Our mind and soul are full of hate and confusion.

Ahmad Al-Khatat

The soldier said: if you shoot me dead now,
My beloved will weep till she gets blind with
The wind till she finds the scent of my flesh.

The fighter said: and if you shoot me now
Martyrs will have joy and the sky will drop
Of joyful rain, upon the homes of darkness.

The soldier said: the farmer can hold and
Be patient for a greater year with more grains,
So, I think is the time to change for good.

The fighter pulled the trigger and shot
His mind to die, while the soldier started
Digging a grave to this fighter so before

The hungry dogs and wolves eat his body,
And gladly it was not the last dialog before
Before killing Iraq, and Iraqis are always powerful.

When Men Fall in Love

Isn't it sad, when men fall in love,
They start ignoring who they are,
Flipping over the clouds of future.

While some haven't seen love near,
They are still healing world wounds,
And their past still destroys present.

In my city, couples walk and talk happy.
Like two love birds flying far as joyfully,
They lose it, when they walk separately.

While in Baghdad women weep by doors,
Sing sad songs like a dove fly with blood,
And smile if she finds her man grave tomb.

I may be alive in front of your beautiful eyes,
Smiling so Baghdad wounds won't appear,
Canadian appreciates my fight against terrorism.

I ask and I seek for a true love for many times,
Apparently, I aged to the autumn tree in spring,
Where women kept on judging as I am blinded.

Angels have asked me to be patient and calm,
When teenagers start becoming worthless actors,
And mothers and daughters are twins for sales.

Ahmad Al-Khatat

Even some have more tattoos than a serial killer,
And men are becoming the dolls of Barbie men,
Sharing their desires with anyone and not worry.

Sadly, the best women, and the most unique ones.
They are dating the trouble of alcohol and all drugs,
While their men kept on creating more horrible sins.

Life is beautiful and amazing,
Life is young and very short,
Life is now miserable and terrifying.

Whenever I ignore a young age homeless on the sidewalk,
I feel I just refuse to open the cage of freedom to an orphan.
Like when I see a little girl, asking her father with less income.

To buy an expensive cake, it recalls me of the girl who wanted
Nothing but her father for the day of the holiday season and
It happens that he died, and her gift from him it's crying alone.

When men fall in love, that is fine and great to see new faces.
But don't accept the scent of spring break into your own life,
Perhaps death has a room, in your life and in your own house.

I Am Not a Poet

I am not a poet and I admit it that I lied about it,
I have been written of my forgotten soul memories.

Selfishness have been taking over my passions,
When I was burning my hopes and all dreams down.

I am not a poet, nor a writer who loves to read.
But I have always wanted to be friends with chapters.

Depression changes my life from sunny to clouds.
Whenever, I dance around the graveyard on a rainy day.

I am not a poet; the crying kid still weeps whenever
He hears the nightingale singing to my painful miseries.

People walk next to my heart and run away quickly.
Before I die and be the tree who dies twice in one year.

I am not a poet, isolated from friends, and unloved.
Although if I am drunk, I feel she's playing hide and seek.

I lost my childhood when my grandpa died within a
Santa clause suit, on the next day to Christmas Eve.

I am not a poet; I have made a necklace with beads of
Names of all the people I love so I recall their kindness.

As time goes by those people walk to the sinful street,
They steal, and they pray asking God for more forgiveness.

I am not a poet, I am rejected from honest and faithful
Love, and I was forced to swallow the cheating and betrayal.

Like if I was born to suffer until I die on your happiest
Day, and fly with broken wings to hell just for being humbled.

I am not a poet, twenty-eight years old seems sixty.
Young face and old heart that will stop at any time sooner.

I could feel everything inside of my flesh but can't
Touch my open wounds but managed to survive very harmfully.

For the Very First Time

For the very first time,
When grief hugged me,
I knew I was an old soul,
Worth noting to anyone.

I died without being loved,
I realized I was just a king,
Without friends or family,
But poetry was my knight.

He was like the dusty book,
Except he writes me down,
While I can't do but crying,
Like a dog running for zero.

I decided to write about you,
Even if you are already hiding,
Or sleeping with somebody else,
Perhaps you will come back.

But you didn't have to go away,
The sea will always be salty as
Your lies and your mankind tears,
Don't waste time with a writer.

Go seek the happy memories,
Where you will be laughing alone,
When you will be loving him more,
Realizing that we were never friends.

Ahmad Al-Khatat

While I spent the nights lonely and
Drunk by the scent of your clothes,
Dancing with the wind of your songs,
Who died once I wrote love songs.

And those songs were playing on,
While a hundred men were touching
And kissing your dirty flesh with a soul
And eyes regretting my pure emotions.

For the very first time, I will dance
And dance with a beautiful wife of
My lifetime, supporting my little girl
To sing of my love and misery songs.

Where the sun and the moon will
Weep without the need of clouds,
Even the birds will learn to appreciate
More than you, since you stabbed love.

When Women Fall in Love

Isn't it sad, when women fall in love,
They dated with the king of death,
They die after giving birth of a baby.

A few hadn't felt the pain of pregnancy,
They are still healing from breast cancer,
And their men haven't been around since.

In my city, couples eat and drink together.
Like two love doves flittering on the nest,
If they ever separate, they fall into miseries.

But in Baghdad women live with pictures,
Those photos are their beloved dead kids,
Who dreamed of attending their wedding.

Women see the darkness before the clouds,
While their men fight until the last breath,
She dreams of pink dreams, reality is miserable.

If my mother smiles my wounds start healing,
Since Baghdad sentenced me to move to exile,
And live and fight against Isis from my pen.

I gave up looking for sweet dreams and love,
Everyone is looking for one night stands for hours,
While my previous woman stabbed me mindlessly.

<u>Ahmad Al-Khatat</u>

Everywhere I travel in this world is much different,
Teenagers start thinking about the old depression,
They are confused about what to love or dislike.

Some warm-hearted women spend time working,
While their men do nothing losing money at casino,
Their girls walk into different rooms making cash.

Sadly, I remember a few women who were writers,
Writing the best novels about love and betrayal,
Realize that betrayal was a true story in lifetime.

Many men say that they are loyal and handsome,
Perhaps they have cheated with widows' women,
And shot the innocent civilians in my country.

This time took me to different unknown directions,
I chose the one to die alone, far from my family,
I dig a grave without creating miseries for them.

When women fall in love, and they say I love you,
To the men, who died of loving them, but they don't
Have enough coins to buy them a giant dull prison.

Colorless Dream

A sinner spirit forced me to sleep,
With my flesh bleeding sins away,
On the pillow of my daily miseries,
And cover me with a dead body.

I close my eyes and my heart too,
I dream with a colorless dream,
Believe me it was not a nightmare,
But a dark journey in my birth city.

Black dust from Baghdad funerals,
White fog to hide the broken wings,
I looked for my childhood house,
I sought the first love of my life.

I forgot to mention that I was blind,
I hear the moaning from the graveyard,
I made a vow to cry my blindness off,
And saw all the rainbow colors on her.

It starts from her golden long hair,
All the way down to her pinky toe,
I asked for a kiss from her red lips,
So, I could stop the flow of blood.

I discovered I was wrong about red,
I saw some women lose their virginity,
It created pleasure into a crime scene.
Two hearts died their emotions innocently.

Ahmad Al-Khatat

Some humans swallow each other's blood,
As if they were a soft drink from a straw,
My age of one hundred years of dusty grief,
It turned into a ten-year innocent child old.

Knowledgeable about everything around me,
I could define the gold digger woman from
The one-night stand lady before going to one,
I have been betrayed and lost the one I loved.

I realized I was the last solider to Free Baghdad,
From all gunmen, and all the mindless terrorists,
With only one old gun within one magical bullet,
Not terrified, but I believe violence brings violence.

I shot my bullet to the black clouds in real life,
To rain swords upon all criminals in this world,
My dreams got the colors back when peace arose,
And I died happily and went flying up to heaven.

The Darkness and the Honey

Tonight, is the darkest night I have ever seen
I am awake as you lie asleep beside me
I keep remembering the sounds of your high heels
as you walked towards me, pulling me into your room.

Trust me when I say you are a very beautiful woman.
Your beauty is what I will savor tonight,
You made me feel so thirsty that I had to drink a cup of water
but the water was drunk by your beauty before I had a chance to sip.

Having you in my bed sharing and raising
The bottle of Jack Daniels whiskey together
But my Jack Daniels has the flavor of honey
but not the same taste of honey I get from kissing your lips.

We both start sharing the same breath
with the same feelings
but with different moves.
We are both enjoying those moments

From your eyes I can see the dark side of romance
I hope you won't close your eyes
because you would make me feel the embers of sorrows
If you open your eyes to snuff out

My embers of sorrows with your tears
then your tears would drop on
My cheeks like an intoxicating remedy.

I'm still awake in an unfathomably deep love
remembering the darkest night
and your sweet honey taste

Ahmad Al-Khatat

Trump Sends Me Back Home

My father once said to my childhood age,
In this great land of America your dreams
Will become real and not miserable like I.

Years later my father is now a grandfather,
I am working as hard as he used to before,
Except I learnt how to be more an American man.

Elections bring sorrows to my thoughts,
It makes my spirit poor then my knowledge,
Weak and uncertain about most of my belief.

God creates most of the humans equally,
Then why those humans aren't equal to me,
Its because my skin color isn't of fall leaves.

The history class should be business class,
The dictionary yearly prints new words to us,
The natives, and black color skin aren't deleted.

Trump wants to send me back home,
After I grew my heart to be an American dude,
I lost my faith and worked in the bloody army.

Trump wants to send my bro home,
His brother died on the dusty border for him,
He wanted a life far from long fights and drugs.

We will see who will build the wall?
Your supporters with fake skin color
And unrealistic names build it with regrets.

Yes, You Are a Terrorist

This life has never
Changed for a bit,

Gadgets devices win
Over manual thinking,

Immigrants' tales aren't
Lies from social network.

Flying bombs in the day;
And fireworks in the night.

Robot soldiers shoot down,
Anyone with a brave heart.

One survivor can't be a zombie,
But he could a deadly terrorist.

Tears and blood are one river,
It tastes the honor of all martyrs.

Bullets and bombs are the fighters,
They don't weep nor speak a word.

Grandparents and single parents,
Orphans and kids in refugee camps.

They sleep with priceless blankets,
Not warm, windy, rainy, and snowy.

Ahmad Al-Khatat

The devil is between the weakness,
Not safe, rape, stealing, and hunger.

Exile accepts them for a better living,
They learn the language, and work hard.

They build one middle class family,
No more hopes to go to homeland.

Their kids are born and love his freedom,
Till one of them becomes responsible.

Because of your own color?
Because of your own name?
Because of your own beliefs?

Opus and congratulations friend,
Unfortunately, you are a terrorist.

Await Your Reply

The last time I heard myself it was when
My thoughts were flying like the butterfly
Below the black moon by the dead clouds
With broken stars and rain died of missing
The farmer who died for planting the planets

My happiness is the weight of a dry leaf
And my sorrow is like the old feelings of
A broken tree with no will to grow heathy
Some many doors are locked and unlocked
A few of them encourage me to go suicide

I stopped drinking water to drink alcohol
I stopped smoking cigarettes to use drugs
I stopped remembering friends to die alone
I stopped laughing to cry and weep bloods
I even stopped learning about my lonesome

Feeling empty and unable to weep with tears
No place or corner to hide from people talking
Nobody wants to respect me and be my friend
You may have some promises to work on them
Just recall that God will see respond to you with

Await your reply……

Ahmad Al-Khatat

Help Me...

Am I growing up mentally or am I suffering emotionally,
Is it the time to change of who I am with you in my mind.

Wake me, I am unable to walk away from my nightmares,
Without holding your warm hands, and feel the paradise.

Wake me, will you dig out my last breath off the ground,
Wake me, and stay with me under the shade of the sun.

Suffer me, I am not the same gamer and heart breaker,
Suffer me, and tie me with the mountain of depressions.

Positive me, from my negative pain of my head to my toe.
Positive me, wipe my my tears when I cried recalling you.

Write me, and feel how the pen dances when you rhyme.
Write me, and look at our pictures and feel my love beats.

Help me, to unlock my soul from the lock of life depression.
Help me, and the sun raises up and upon all over wounded.

Love me, and take my heart as your gold chain on your neck,
Love me, and break my shyness and let my lips say I love you.

Kiss me, and don't weep more of tears that will push me away.
Kiss me, so I live a second life worthwhile to have you with me.

My favourite has been the graveyard for the past dark years.
Will you open your eyes, and take me to your heart before I die.

Love on the War's Frontline

You may think I am twenty six young loving heart beats old,
But I am one hundred sorrows years old of my time left to hope.

I will unlock my door to you, and wait for you again and again.
Remember my age is depending on those last burning candles.

I Am Sorry…
I will always love you the most

Ahmad Al-Khatat

What Will Remain

What will remain of me today or the coming year, will it be worth a bird's feather
The only grief in my bloodroot is the sad song of nightingales like a wedding with a mother in a picture frame
In this life I could live foolishly and lost in problems with a place in darkness to weep till I die
The tattooist of previous wars asked me about my homeland I told him that I was sold to the land of happiness
With a friend who broke my trust, a woman who died before loving me, and parents who denied my existence
What will remain of me, not an expensive pen, but an unreadable diary of the depths of my soul

They Broke Me and Not My Heart

The sun shines in a friendly way
and I am looking for another way
to hide or show my feelings after
they broke me and not my heart

Call me Mr. lonely depressed who
deserves nothing but to stay awake
with no falling tears, instead biting
my tongue for trusting this world

This is not the blue skies up there
I want a painter to draw a cloud
to bury myself a grave far from the
guilty ones, near to the dead roses

I wish if I was a victim to die instead of
seeing faces whom I want to drown
in the bottom of the deep river mercilessly;
even mercy no longer has a space in me

My tears have always been tasteless
therefore, I do not find anything is sweet
or worthy to choose which house, car, and
even a watch to buy from the dust of this world.

Ahmad Al-Khatat

I Have One Kiss

I have one kiss to my religious prophet
Who offer me a religion in forgiveness
And peace with myself and to others
I am who I am I love you for the way
You are and not the way others judge
You for the freedom of speech they own

I have one kiss to the running tears
For making some of my dreams true
For offering me a beautiful woman
Who taught me a lot about myself
Who showed me the realistic me
And stopped me from digging a hole

I have one kiss to my lifetime queen
For making the rain into a symbol for
Bliss and blessings and not a day worth
My death and creating above my mind
A little daughter running 'tween the borders
Of Guatemala and Iraq happy forever

I have one kiss to the writer about love
For making him into a sweet and pure
Tree with green branches and loving
Fruits to taste and making alcohol to
Drink all the leaves to get drunk later
And wake up with a bigger sunny smile

Love on the War's Frontline

I have one kiss to the sea of no regrets
And mini kisses to the grain of salt in it
Who help the refugees to sail safer and
alive to a greater land to their little kids
And adults as well, and leave their worth
To start a life facing the face of racism

I have one kiss to the church and temple
For letting me praying to my God without
Holding weapons behind my head with a
Question if I am Christian, Jew or Muslim
And accepting me the way I am myself and
Didn't ask me questions to change my believe

Ahmad Al-Khatat

Love in the War Frontline...

Growing up without parents
Nor step brother or step sister;
It creates an empty space inside
The heart, the mind, and the soul.

The graveyard said that I used
To sleep between two old tombs
On the right it was for a solider
And to the left it was his beloved.

I slept and thought they were
My parents. I talked with them
And always tasted in my dreams
My mother's Breast milk to smile for a day

My story is too dull to be shared
Some will cry and do nothing
Others would give some tips
And nobody offers me a small hope

I became friends with spirits
Most of them weren't orphans
We played so many fun times
Bombs and bullets weren't included

So many wars in my world
Rainbow appeared in movies
So much smoke and blood
were the only ones in my fantasies

Love on the War's Frontline

Girls are locked in lockers
The keys are with enemies
Bleeding one for every hour
Sucking it till the spirit flies to heaven

Freedom, is not a word
Peace, is not a word either
History, it's a book of lies
Written by leaders and brain washers

Luck died with younger kids
Bad luck died by the widows
The sun arises with fall tears
To rain in winter to clean the views

Love in the war frontline
Was seen in more movies
My life it's real like the rose
Never dies to kiss the death and die

Ahmad Al-Khatat

I Am Sorry Baghdad

I am sorry Baghdad, but I have to travel,
I will be back in years in a wooden box.

The television doesn't show the freedom,
The radio station talks about unsure hopes.

I am sitting on a fancy brown leather sofa,
It feels as if I am sitting on an old wheelchair.

Tears it's an old way to express my yearnings,
My memories were lost in a boat of fishermen.

I smile to hide my cuts of feeling homesickness,
I weep to show my joys of having a citizenship.

Everybody look at their gadgets but not myself,
I am still seeking to meet with an angel from Iraq.

Perhaps maybe she could be the mother of kids,
Picking them before the ground crush them down.

I asked the taxi driver to get me to Baghdad station,
He replied, that will be the last station on the death line.

In my whole life, I have been drunk only two times,
First when I died in in Baghdad, and other was

When I knew Baghdad can't offer a bit of myself,
I am sorry Baghdad to be your armless soldier.

Ahmad Al-Khatat was born in Baghdad, Iraq. His work has appeared in print globally and he has poems translated into several languages. He has previously been nominated for the *Best of the Net* awards. He lives in Canada.

colophon

Love on the War's Frontline, by Ahmad Al-Khatat,
was set with Trebuchet MS fonts
by SpiNDec, Port Saint Lucie, Florida.
The jacket and covers were designed by
Kris Haggblom, Port Saint Lucie, Florida.
The cover art is by Julia Stuart.

www.ingramcontent.com/pod-product-compliance
Lightning Source LLC
Chambersburg PA
CBHW030104100526
44591CB00008B/266